WILDWORLD

Elephants

Karen Dudley

A & C Black · London

This edition published 1999 in Great Britain by
A & C Black (Publishers) Ltd, 35 Bedford Row, London WC1R 4JH
First published 1997 in Canada by Weigl Educational Publishers Limited.

ISBN 0-7136-5132-6
A Cataloguing in Publication Data (CIP) record of this book is available from the British Library.

Printed and bound in Canada

Project Editor
Lauri Seidlitz

Design and Illustration
Warren Clark

Project Coordinator
Amanda Woodrow

Editor
Kathy DeVico

Copyeditor
Janice Parker

Layout
Chris Bowerman

Consultants

Louise Charlton, Kenya Wildlife Fund

Dr Ronald Orenstein, Project Director, International Wildlife Coalition

Dr E. Melanie Watt, Wildlife Zoologist

Acknowledgments
The publisher wishes to thank Warren Rylands for inspiring this series.

Special thanks to IUCN-The World Conservation Union, The African Wildlife Foundation, and Brian Keating of the Calgary Zoo

Contents

Introduction

Elephants are one of the most unusual-looking animals in the world.

Elephants frequently take baths. Baths help elephants keep cool in the hot sun.

Elephants are known for their large size, strength, and great intelligence. Their name comes from the Greek word *elaph,* which means "ivory". Elephants are also one of the most unusual-looking animals in the world. They have many special adaptations to help them survive in their environment.

Much of what we know about elephants is from studies done on elephants living in the East African grasslands. In this book, you will learn a great deal about these elephants. You will find out how these large creatures can move quietly through a forest. You will also learn why elephants plaster themselves with mud. Follow along as elephants travel through forests, deserts, and grasslands in their constant search for food and water.

Features

The single feature that really distinguishes elephants from other animals is their trunk.

Opposite: One of the ways that elephants can be identified is by the shape and size of their tusks.

An elephant uses its trunk as a nose, an arm, and a hand. It has about 150,000 muscles!

N o other animal looks quite like an elephant, and there is a good reason for this. Elephants are a unique group of mammals with few close relatives. Elephants are the largest living land mammal. You might think that an animal as big as an elephant would move very slowly. Elephants cannot jump, but they can easily outrun a human.

The single feature that really distinguishes elephants from other animals is their trunk. Elephants use their trunk for so many things, that it is essential to an elephant's survival. If an elephant's trunk is badly injured, it will likely die.

Classification

There are only two species of elephants living today, the African elephant (*Loxodonta africana*) and the Asian elephant (*Elephas maximus*). Elephants are related to the extinct mammoths and mastodons, large elephant-like creatures that mostly died out over 10,000 years ago. Today, the elephant's closest living relatives are hyraxes and sea cows. Hyraxes are small furry animals that live in rain forests in Africa and rocky areas in Africa and the Middle East. Sea cows, such as manatees and dugongs, live in subtropical oceans. The common ancestor of elephants, hyraxes, and sea cows lived over 50 million years ago.

Even though hyraxes look a lot like guinea pigs, the structure of their teeth, limbs, and feet are more similar to elephants and sea cows.

SUBSPECIES

There are two subspecies of the African elephant and three subspecies of the Asian elephant. The elephants are divided into subspecies based on characteristics such as size, skin colour, and the size and shape of their ears.

Species	Latin Name	Where They Live
African Elephant	*Loxodonta africana africana*	African **savannas**
	Loxodonta africana cyclotis	African forests
Asian Elephant	*Elephas maximus indicus*	Asian mainland
	Elephas maximus maximus	Sri Lanka
	Elephas maximus sumatranus	Sumatra

Size

The size of a full grown elephant depends on its gender and where it lives. Below is a chart of the average adult size of different subspecies of elephants. Males are larger than females of the same age. Females tend to be at the smaller end of the range provided, and males tend to be at the larger end. Male elephants grow throughout their lives, while females reach their largest size when they are about 20 years old. A large male elephant can weigh as much as three small vans.

Elephants have the largest and heaviest brains of all land mammals. The brain of an adult elephant weighs about 4.5 kg. An average adult human brain weighs only 1.4 kg.

The tallest elephant ever recorded stood 4 metres high at the shoulders. The heaviest elephant ever recorded weighed about 11,340 kg!

HEIGHT AND WEIGHT

Subspecies	Height	Weight
African Elephant (Bush)	3–4 metres	4,000–7,000 kg
African Elephant (Forest)	2–3 metres	2,000–4,500 kg
Asian Elephant (Sri Lanka)	2–3.5 metres	2,000–5,500 kg
Asian Elephant (Asia Mainland)	2–3.5 metres	2,000–5,000 kg
Asian Elephant (Sumatra)	2–3.2 metres	2,000–4,000 kg

African vs. Asian Elephants

African and Asian elephants look somewhat different. Here are a few ways you can tell the two kinds of elephants apart:

AFRICA

African

- Swaybacked
- Large ears
- Smooth, flat forehead
- Both males and females have tusks.
- Two "fingers" at tip of trunk
- More pronounced ridges on trunk

Looking at an elephant's ears is a good way to figure out where the elephant comes from. The ears of an African elephant are large and shaped like the continent of Africa. An Asian elephant has smaller ears that are shaped like India.

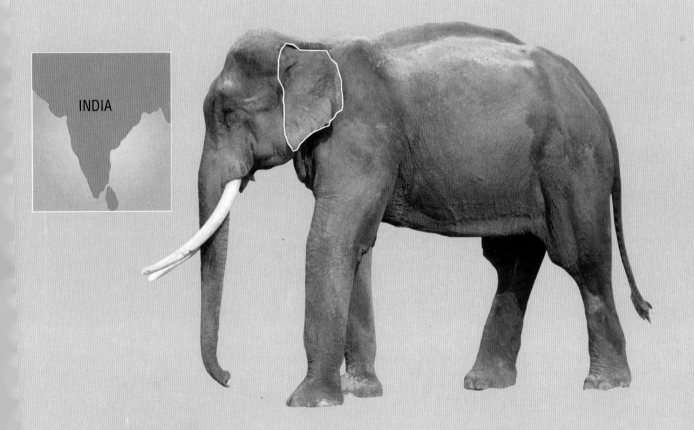

INDIA

Asian

- Level or rounded back
- Small ears
- Two bumps on forehead
- Tusks on females cannot easily be seen or are absent.

- One "finger" at tip of trunk
- Smoother trunk

Special Adaptations

Elephants have several unique features that help them survive in their environment.

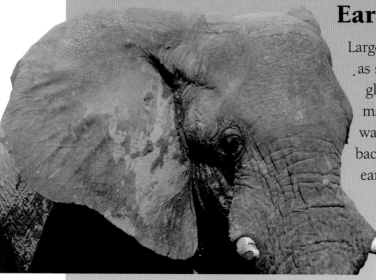

Elephant ears help biologists study elephants. Elephants usually have holes or small tears on the edges of their ears in a pattern that is unique to each elephant. These nicks and holes help biologists to identify individual elephants.

Ears

Large ears help keep elephants cool. As far as scientists can tell, elephants have no sweat glands. Biologists believe that elephants may keep cool by spraying themselves with water, taking a bath, or by flapping their ears back and forth. The blood vessels in their ears are very close to the surface of the skin. Some of these vessels are very large. As an elephant flaps its ears, the air cools the blood in the vessels. This cooled blood then flows back into the rest of the body to cool off the elephant. This cooling process allows elephants to live in a climate that may be very hot and dry. The ears of an adult African bush elephant are about 1.8 metres long and almost 1.5 metres wide. Asian elephants have smaller ears than the African species.

Legs and Feet

Elephants have strong legs and specially adapted feet to support their massive weight. Although their feet look flat, elephants actually walk on the tips of their toes. Each foot has a layer of fatty padding between the toes and on the soles. When the elephant puts its weight on its foot, the padding helps absorb the shock. This thick cushioning allows an elephant to walk quietly, in spite of its large size.

Elephants usually walk at a rate of 5 kilometres per hour. They can run at speeds of up to 40 kilometres per hour.

Tusks and Teeth

Elephant tusks are actually very long teeth. Elephants have one pair of tusks that grows throughout their lives. These special teeth wear down with use. Tusks are visible on adult African elephants and all male Asian elephants. The tusks of female Asian elephants are sometimes missing or so small that they cannot easily be seen. An adult African bull elephant can have tusks up to 3.4 metres long. This is as long as he is tall!

The shape of an elephant's tusks is unique. Most elephants use one tusk more than the other. Just like humans are right- or left-handed, elephants are right- or left-tusked. This is why the tusks of some elephants look a little lopsided. The tusk that is used more often wears down faster.

Elephants also have large, flat teeth that they use to chew their food. When these grinding teeth are worn down, they are replaced by others. The new teeth grow in from behind the existing teeth, much like a conveyor belt. This happens six times during an elephant's lifetime. The last set of teeth comes in when the elephant is about 40 years old. During its life, an elephant will have a total of only 26 teeth, including its tusks.

In order to support heavy tusks and a muscular trunk, an elephant's skull must be very thick. As you can see from this diagram, the skull is filled with air spaces so the elephant's head is not too heavy.

An elephant's teeth are highly ridged for chewing on tough vegetation.

Trunk

One of the elephant's most amazing features is its long trunk. The Swahili word for trunk is *mkono*, which means "hand". The trunk is both an elephant's hand and arm. It has no bones, and contains about 150,000 muscles. All these muscles allow the elephant to twist and bend its trunk in all directions. The trunk can lift an elephant calf from a deep mudhole or pick a single leaf from a tree. On the tip of their trunks, elephants have flexible "fingers". Asian elephants have one finger, and African elephants have two fingers. To pick something up, the Asian elephant pinches its finger against the lower tip of its trunk, and the African elephant pinches its two fingers together.

The trunk is also a nose and upper lip. Elephants breathe with their trunks, and have a good sense of smell. Using their trunks, elephants can smell the air for water or food, or to tell if a predator is nearby.

Elephants also use their trunks to eat, drink, trumpet, and communicate. They can also suck up water or dust to give themselves a shower. Elephants also greet, touch, and show affection to other family members with their trunks. They can rub their own eyes and ears, and may even use their trunks to pick up small sticks to scratch an itch or to flick off ticks. An elephant's trunk is very important to its survival.

Elephants are excellent swimmers. They can even cross wide rivers without much difficulty, often using their trunks as snorkels.

Skin

An elephant's baggy-looking skin can be up to an 25 mm thick in some places. Although this skin is tough enough to protect the elephant from sharp thorns and stinging insects, it is still very sensitive.

Most elephants are quite hairy at birth, especially on their backs and heads. As the elephants grow older, the amount of hair decreases to a few dark, bristly hairs around the eyes, ear openings, chin, and on the tail. This hair is not enough to protect them from the sun. Elephants often plaster themselves with a coating of mud to prevent their skin from drying out, cracking, or burning. The mud also helps to protect them from insect bites. Mudholes, or **wallows**, are a favourite place for elephants to gather. Sometimes they roll around in the mud to cover themselves. Elephants may also bathe in a river or a stream before spraying dust over themselves. The dust combines with the water to form a mudpack over their skin. Clean elephants are dark grey in colour. When they coat themselves with mud and dust, they take on the colour of the soil where they live.

An elephant's wrinkly skin helps cool the elephant by trapping moisture in the creases.

LIFE SPAN

An elephant can live for up to 65 years in the wild. By this time, the elephant's last set of teeth have worn down, and it is unable to eat properly. Eventually the elephant dies of malnutrition and related diseases. Like many other wild animals, elephants face many dangers. Often elephants die before they even reach old age. In drought years, many elephants die of starvation. The death rate of calves is especially high at these times. Other dangers include accidents and injuries, heart and blood diseases, and hunting by people.

The Family Unit

Biologists learned that family units are not led by a bull elephant, but by the oldest female in the group.

Opposite: A typical elephant family unit is made up of related cows and their calves.

Scientists once believed that wild elephants lived in groups that were led by the largest bull elephant. However, at that time, nobody really knew how elephants lived or how they communicated with one another.

In the late 1950s, a few biologists decided to find out more about wild elephants. They started to study the groups in East Africa, and have since learned a lot about African savanna elephants.

As biologists studied the elephants, they discovered that a family unit is made up of female elephants and their calves. They learned that family units are not led by a bull elephant, but by the oldest female in the group. They also learned that elephants have many ways of communicating with one another.

Young calves are rarely without the protection and care of one or more adults.

Composition

A typical elephant family unit is made up of 3 to 25 members. Usually the members are mothers and their calves, and other related females.

The family unit grows in size when younger cows have their own calves. If a family unit grows too large, some of the elephants may split off to form their own group. Often a family unit stays close to one to five other related family units. These related family units are known as **bond groups**. If two of these family units lose members to disease or **poaching**, they may join again to form a single family unit. Several bond groups that share the same **home range** are known as a **clan**.

Each family unit is led by the oldest cow, known as a **matriarch**. She decides when the family will travel, and where they will stop to eat and rest. She watches out for danger, and makes the decision to charge or flee. A matriarch is usually 40 to 50 years old. During her long life, she has learned a lot. She knows the best feeding areas and remembers where the best water holes can be found. A matriarch leads her family unit until she dies. When this happens, her place is taken by the next oldest female.

An elephant family unit usually keeps its calves safely protected in the centre of the group.

An African bull will sometimes charge another wild animal or human if it feels threatened. An African elephant about to attack will lift its head, wrap its trunk around its tusk so that it is out of the way, and spread and flap its ears quickly. The elephant pictured here is alarmed, but is only bluffing to scare off an intruder.

Bull Elephants

Unlike female elephants, adult male elephants do not live in family units. When male elephants are 10 to 15 years old, they are usually ready to leave their family groups. Exactly when an elephant leaves depends on the individual elephant involved. Some mature faster than others. After leaving his family unit, a bull might tag along with another family unit for a few years. Some young males may even follow another bull. As a young bull gets older, he will spend more time with the other bulls in the bull area. The bull area is a place where male elephants gather to test their strength and establish their rank. This is done through **sparring matches**. Smaller, weaker bulls give way to the larger, stronger ones.

An adult male elephant either travels alone, or with one or two other bulls. When he is ready to mate, the bull will travel with a family unit for a while. An adult bull stays with a family unit only if he wants to mate, and only if there is a female elephant that is also ready to mate.

Seasonal Activities

In most places where elephants live in the wild, there are two main seasons—the wet season and the dry season. A family unit's seasonal movements, or **migrations**, are affected by these seasons. During the dry season, little or no rain falls. Elephants try to spend their days around water holes, rivers, and other sources of water. At night, when it is cooler, they move into more open areas to look for food. Food is scarce at this time, so bond groups seldom get together. They must spread out so they can find enough to eat.

With the onset of the rainy season, elephants start to get restless. The land will soon be covered with tender grasses, herbs, and shrubs. As the new vegetation grows, the elephants migrate to the savannas and forests to find the best food. Bond groups begin to come together. Sometimes clans of over 400 elephants gather together if the rainfall has been heavy and there is enough food for everyone.

African elephants feed in swampy areas during the dry season. As soon as it rains, most of the elephants move to higher ground to eat the more nutritious plants growing in the soil.

Communication

Elephants rumble, trumpet, gurgle, and screech as they communicate with one another. In addition, biologists had observed that distant groups of elephants seemed to be able to coordinate their behaviour, even when the groups were out of hearing range. Some people speculated that elephants used telepathic methods to communicate. In 1986 biologists discovered that elephants communicate using very low-pitched sounds, known as **infrasonic sounds**. These sounds are so low that humans cannot hear them. Biologists can hear these calls only by recording the sounds with special equipment and playing the sounds back at ten times the normal speed. In the open bush country, elephants can hear these infrasonic calls from up to 10 kilometres away. This discovery explained a lot about elephant communication.

Body language plays an important role in elephant communication. The ways an elephant holds its head, its trunk, and its ears all have certain meanings. When elephants are excited or happy, they flap their ears. When elephants face danger, they lift their heads and spread their ears. This may make them seem larger and more threatening.

Elephants can also communicate through scent. A female attracts mates because her urine has a certain smell when she is ready to mate. Elephants also have a certain odour when they are sick, or when they are about to give birth. This helps other elephants know when their family unit members might need help.

An elephant may spread its ears and lift its trunk high in the air to smell its surroundings, especially if something alarms or excites it.

Elephant Relationships

Elephants form close, loyal, lifelong attachments with members of their families. Elephant societies are highly organized. Family unit members usually eat, drink, and rest within a few yards of one another.

Greetings

During the day, individual family unit members may wander off or spread out to find food. As soon as the family unit comes together again, the elephants happily greet one another by screeching, flapping their ears, and rumbling loudly. When bond groups come together, the rumbling, trumpeting, and screeching can be very loud. Elephants also greet each other by winding their trunks together. An elephant greets special friends or family members by putting the tip of its trunk into the other elephant's mouth.

Elephants express their attachment for one another through frequent physical contact.

Helping

Elephants are very supportive of one another. If one elephant is sick or injured, its family unit members try to help it. They soothe it with caresses, and slow down so the wounded elephant can keep up with them. If the elephant cannot move, the other family members use their trunks and tusks to try to keep it standing. If it has fallen down, they try to pull it to its feet. Sometimes they even bring food to a weak or dying elephant.

Elephants are fascinated with elephant bones. One biologist reported that elephants even came into her camp at night to remove the elephant jaws she had collected for her work.

Elephants and Death

One of the most mysterious things about elephants is their reaction to death. When an elephant dies, other elephants do not move on right away. Mother elephants may stay with their dead calves for days, long after the rest of the family has left. After some time, elephants turn away from the dead elephant. Elephants have been observed touching the dead animal lightly with their feet before continuing on their way. Sometimes they cover the body with grasses, dirt, or branches before leaving the area.

Elephants can recognise the skeletons of other elephants. They ignore the bones of other animals, but as soon as a family unit comes across the bones of an elephant, they grow quiet and tense. They inspect the skeleton carefully, feeling and stroking the bones with the tips of their trunks, or turning them over with their feet.

Sometimes elephants pick up the bones and carry them away. Special attention is given to the skull bones and tusks. Some biologists think that the elephants may be trying to identify the dead elephant. In a few cases, elephants have even pulled the tusks out from elephant skeletons and scattered them.

Elephant Calves

At birth, an elephant calf is totally dependent on its mother and the other family unit members.

Opposite: All adult members of a family unit guard calves from danger.

While learning to use its trunk, a calf can spend hours at a time picking up sticks and exploring everything.

For the first 10 to 12 years of their lives, young elephants are carefully protected and nurtured by their family unit. At birth, an elephant calf is totally dependent on its mother and the other family unit members. A calf is usually able to stand within an hour of its birth, but it cannot defend itself. The rest of the family unit slows down so the calf can keep up with it. Older sisters and half-sisters are especially caring. They often protect and play with the calf as if it were their own.

As the calves follow their mothers, they slowly learn what to eat, where to drink, and how to avoid danger. Elephants have a long period of development and learning. Living in a family unit gives calves the protection and care they need while they learn how to survive.

Mating

Most elephants mate during the rainy season. At this time, they are strong and healthy after eating fresh grasses and herbs. Females are ready to mate from about 12 years of age. A female will not have a second calf until her first calf has been **weaned**. A cow may have about 7 calves during her lifetime.

Bull elephants are usually ready to mate at about 12 years of age. Between 25 to 35 years of age, bulls begin to enter **musth**. When a bull is in musth, he is especially eager to mate. Musth usually happens once a year for each bull, although they can also mate at other times. Bulls may enter musth at different times. This helps prevent conflicts between bulls over females.

Calves

The **gestation** period for elephants is 18–22 months. An elephant mother usually gives birth to a single calf. If twins are born, usually only one survives. About 99 per cent of elephant calves are born at night.

When an elephant is ready to give birth, she drops back from the rest of the family unit. Often a female relative stays with the mother during the birth and helps the calf once it is born. Newborn elephants weigh about 118 kilograms and are less than a metre tall at the shoulder. They are born with tight, curly black or red hair on their foreheads. New calves may not be able to see very well, so they usually identify their mothers by touch, scent, and sound.

This African elephant calf is less than one hour old. For the next few months, it will stay within a few feet of its mother's protection.

Care

During the first few months of its life, an elephant calf stays very close to its mother. The mother watches her calf closely, and is ready to help if it gets stuck in mud or caught in a tangle of grass. The calf suckles often, bending its little trunk out of the way to drink with its mouth. Calves continue to suckle until they are three to four years old. Male calves tend to demand more milk. They are also usually weaned later than female calves.

When calves are about six months old, they start to eat plants. Even though they can eat solid food at this time, they still need to drink the same amount of milk. Calves learn which foods are good to eat by reaching up to their mother's mouth and pulling out a piece of whatever she is chewing.

Older sisters and older female relatives are very important to a new elephant calf. These young females are very interested in the new family unit member. They guard the calf from danger, and bring it back if it wanders off. They also play with it and feed it, allowing the mother to feed and rest. By taking care of the calf, a young female learns how to take proper care of her own young. When she has her own calf, she will be a good mother. Cows who look after calves that are not their own are called **allomothers**. The only thing allomothers cannot do is nurse the calf. If the mother elephant is killed, the calf dies of dehydration.

Even though a calf is able to eat plant food by the time it is six months old, it still needs the nutrition provided by its mother's milk. The mother's large body also provides warmth and protection from poor weather.

Development

Birth – 1 year

A newborn calf is almost totally helpless. After a few hours, it can stand and feed, but its legs are shaky, and it cannot run or walk very far.

Calves are born curious. They must learn almost everything by watching, exploring, and experimenting. They spend a lot of time smelling and touching as they explore their environment. Young calves do not seem to know what to do with their trunks. They often stand and just whirl or wiggle them around. Sometimes a calf may even trip over its own trunk. Calves this young do not even know how to drink with their trunks. In spite of these troubles, calves use their trunks to comfort themselves. Just as a human baby sucks its thumb, an elephant calf sucks its trunk.

By 6–8 months, it begins to use its trunk to drink and feed itself. The calf still drops a lot of food and water in the process, but it keeps practising. After about six months, the calf's fuzzy hair is replaced by stiff, black bristles. The calf is still very dependent on its mother and stays close to her for protection. During this time, calves play together a lot. This helps them learn the social skills necessary for life in the family unit.

Young elephants play together frequently. Their games often include running at each other and butting heads, or chasing one another and grabbing tails with their trunks.

1 year – 12 years

Calves are now much better at using their trunks. They can keep up with the family unit fairly well, and they are very playful. When they are around two years old, their tusks begin to appear. Most elephants are weaned by the time they are about three or four years old.

After about four years, the calves are no longer as dependent on their mothers, but they still need the protection and care of the family unit. During this time, they learn how to survive. Young cows may become allomothers, and young bulls begin to wander off from their family unit. By age 10–15, a young male has usually left the group, while a young cow may be ready to have a calf of her own.

By the end of their first year, most calves have learned to control and use their trunks like the old bull pictured here.

Habitat

During the dry season, when food and water are scarce, a family unit's range may double in size.

Opposite: A family unit may use the same bathing and drinking sites over many generations.

lephants need a lot of space to live, but the ideal elephant habitat needs to have much more than lots of space. Elephants need places where they can find grasses, trees, herbs, and shrubs to eat. They need a good source of water to drink, and streams or pools in which to bathe. They also need wallows to roll in so their skin is protected from stinging insects. The size of a family unit's home range depends on how many of these things are available. Sometimes elephants can find everything they need in a small area. Other times, they may have to travel for many miles to find enough food or water. During the dry season, when food and water are scarce, a family unit's home range may double in size.

Both African and Asian elephants live in a variety of habitats. These include savannas, forests, marshy areas, and lake shores. Some African bush elephants even live in the desert.

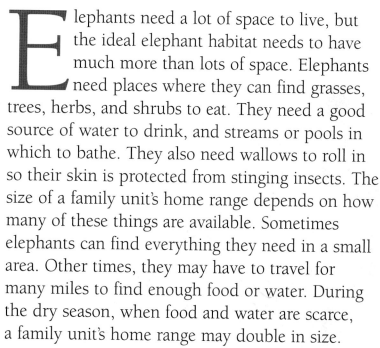

As elephants travel across their home range, they often leave wide paths behind. Sometimes these "elephant highways" come together to connect wallows, drinking pools, favourite feeding areas, and dust bathing sites, such as the one shown in this photograph.

Architects of their Environment

Elephants play an important role in the health of their ecosystems. They can help create habitats for other plants and animals. Their role includes clearing pathways, opening up new water holes, and spreading seeds. In their search for food, they rip off strips of tree bark with their tusks, and tear down branches to get at the leaves. Broken branches, fruit, and twigs feed smaller creatures. Sometimes they even push over entire trees. As the trees in a forest are knocked down by elephants, grasses and other plants that need a lot of sunlight can grow. As elephants constantly munch on larger shrubs, bush growth is controlled so that smaller plants have a chance to thrive. **Clearings** in a forest provide homes for other animals.

Elephants are very good at finding water during the dry season. They have such a good sense of smell that they can find underground water sources. By digging deep with their tusks and feet, they bring the water to the surface. In this way, they provide a source of drinking water for other animals.

Even the dung that elephants leave behind changes their environment. Much of what an elephant eats is not digested. An elephant feeding on fruits in the forest may wander onto the plain before depositing its dung. Fruit seeds in the dung then take root and grow, creating a new group of trees. One study, conducted in Africa, found that 21 different plant species were spread by elephants in this way.

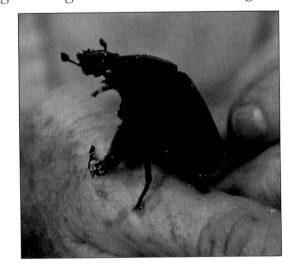

Some creatures, such as the dung beetle, depend upon elephants for their survival. The dung beetle eats undigested plant material in elephant droppings.

Viewpoints

Should elephants be kept in zoos?

An elephant is one of the most popular animals at a zoo. People are drawn to its large size, gentle personality, and unusual appearance. Should we keep elephants in zoos just because we like to look at them? Are zoos prisons where elephants are forced to live in unnatural conditions, or are they a protected place for an endangered species?

PRO

1 Breeding elephants in zoos can help to protect the **genetic diversity** of the elephant species. If wild elephant populations either die out or are drastically reduced, elephants from the captive programmes can be used to re-establish the wild populations.

2 In zoos, elephants are protected from poachers and other dangers. Zoo elephants always have enough to eat, and they always have medical care.

3 An important part of elephant conservation involves educating people about them. Zoo elephants play an important role in education. After admiring a zoo elephant, people may work harder to save elephants in the wild.

CON

1 Elephants breed very slowly and require a lot of space, so it would be very difficult for zoos to breed enough elephants to save the species. Although North American zoos have successfully bred Asian elephants, they have not been able to breed the African species.

2 Captive elephants do not lead a natural life. Elephants raised in zoos cannot learn how to use their natural habitat. Learned behaviours passed down from generation to generation will be lost.

3 Elephants are very intelligent creatures. They are easily bored and frustrated. Although zoos often provide as much stimulation as they can, elephants need to live with their family units in much larger spaces than a zoo can provide.

Food

Elephants spend 16 hours of their day either eating or looking for food.

Opposite: Elephants living in the savanna often seem to prefer the tall, tough grasses that other herbivores do not eat.

Elephants are **herbivores**, which means they are plant-eaters. Adult elephants have huge appetites, sometimes eating over 136 kilograms of food in one day. It takes a long time and a lot of effort to find so much to eat. Elephants spend 16 hours of their day either eating or looking for food.

Elephants have a wide range of foods from which to choose. What they eat depends on the kinds of foods available in their habitat. Their diet may consist of over 400 species of plants, including acacia seeds and bark, palm trees, and a variety of grasses, herbs, and shrubs. Elephants are very fond of certain tree species, and they may eat the bark, leaves, and fruit from those trees. Their favourite foods include wild fruits and berries.

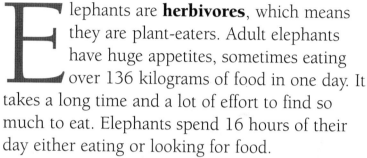

An elephant drinks by sucking water into its trunk and releasing it into its mouth. Elephants cannot use their trunks as straws any more than you can use your nose as a straw.

How They Eat

Elephants do not eat constantly throughout the day. In between feedings, they take time to travel, socialise, relax, digest, or cool off in a bath.

When they are feeding, elephants use their tusks, trunks, and feet. They peel the bark off trees by using their tusks like a chisel. They use their tusks and feet to dig stems and roots from the ground. To eat grasses and herbs, an elephant wraps its trunk around the plants and pulls them out by the roots. If earth comes up with the plants, the elephant shakes the plants against its foot until the soil falls off.

An elephant's height helps it to reach leaves and fruit in tall trees. By resting on its hind legs and lifting its trunk up high, an adult elephant can reach higher than a giraffe. In this way, during times of drought, the elephants can find food even when the grasses have dried out and died.

One of the reasons that elephants need so much food is because half of what they eat passes through their bodies without being digested. In one day, ten well-fed elephants can leave behind 907 kilograms of dung.

By stretching its trunk, an elephant can feed on leaves and twigs that other grazing animals cannot reach. This is especially useful during the dry season when grasses and herbs are scarce.

Although elephants need to eat salt, they cannot use their tongues to lick salty ground or rocks. Elephants therefore use their trunks and tusks to eat salty soil.

Water and Salt

Elephants usually drink only once or twice a day. Sometimes they must travel many miles to find water. An adult can gulp down up to 160 litres of water in a 24-hour period. Calves that have not yet learned to use their trunks drink by kneeling down to a pool and slurping water up with their mouths. An adult drinks by drawing up about 11 litres of water into its trunk, curling its trunk around, and spraying the water into its mouth.

Like other animals, elephants also need salt to survive. When soils lack minerals, the plants that grow in these soils also lack minerals. Often the plants that elephants eat contain very few minerals such as salt. Whenever elephants feel hungry for salt, they search for salty soil or rock. Using their tusks, elephants loosen the soil or rock before picking up the pieces and eating them.

On Mount Elgon, in Kenya, there is a cave called Kitum that is 160 metres deep, 40 metres wide, and 4 metres high. Elephants go into this cave to dig for salt. As the cave is almost totally dark inside, elephants must use their trunks along the cave walls to feel their way around. Mother elephants lay a protective trunk over their calves so the young elephants do not wander away in the dark. Some scientists believe that this cave was made by generations of elephants digging for salt over thousands of years.

The Food Cycle

A food cycle shows how energy, in the form of food, is passed from one living thing to another. Elephants survive by eating plants. As you can see from the cycle, the African elephant's daily round of feeding and drinking affects the lives of other living things. Many plants and animals depend on elephants to survive. What might happen if elephants disappeared from the cycle?

Elephants push over trees, bringing twigs and leaves down for smaller grazing animals.

As elephants travel, egrets and other birds feed on the insects that the elephants kick up.

Elephants dig water holes, which are used by other animals.

Baboons feed by picking out seeds and insects from elephant dung.

A dead elephant provides food for many scavengers and predators.

Elephant dung provides food for dung beetles, which also lay their eggs in balls of dung.

Seeds in elephant dung sprout in new areas when the dung is deposited.

Wildlife Biologists Talk About Elephants

Cynthia Moss

"My priority, my love, my life are the Amboseli elephants, but I also want to ensure that there are elephants in other places that are able to exist in all the complexity and joy that elephants are capable of. It may be a lot to ask as we are about to enter the twenty-first century, but I think it is a goal worth striving for."

Cynthia Moss has been studying the elephants in Amboseli National Park in Kenya since 1973. She has written many books, including *Elephant Memories: Thirteen Years in the Life of an Elephant Family*, and *Echo of the Elephants*.

Iain Douglas-Hamilton

"When I think of what elephants mean to me I don't just look at them in a scientific way...Here is an animal that can pick you up in her gnarled trunk, hurl you like a cannonball, pierce your body with irresistible force or crush the life out of you, and yet who may equally touch you as tenderly as a mother."

Iain Douglas-Hamilton has been an elephant biologist since the 1960s. He and his wife, Oria, have studied the elephants in Manyara, Tanzania and have written many books, including *Among the Elephants*, and *Battle for the Elephants*.

Ian Redmond

"[The discovery of infrasonic calls] served to remind us that there is still much to learn about elephants. They play a central role in the ecology of Africa and many other species of animals and plants could not survive without them."

Ian Redmond is a biologist who has studied the elephants at Kitum Cave in Mount Elgon National Park, Kenya. He is the author of several articles and books, including *The Elephant Book*, which was written for the elephant protection group called Elefriends.

Competition

Even when food and water are scarce, elephants remain very tolerant of other animals.

Opposite: Although bulls will spar with one another, sparring matches are often just a way to establish rank.

Many different animals live in the forests and grasslands of Africa and Asia. Some, like antelope and buffalo, eat many of the same foods as elephants. There is rarely any direct conflict between elephants and these other animals. Buffalo, impalas, hippopotamuses, and antelope may graze only a few yards away from a group of elephants. Even when food and water are scarce, elephants remain very tolerant of other animals.

Elephants may wrestle or spar with one another occasionally, but violent fighting among them is rare. These gentle giants are so large that

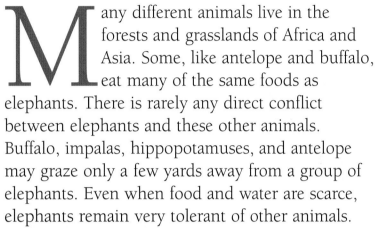

their size usually protects them from being killed and eaten by other animals. Adult elephants have no real enemies or predators, except for humans.

Elephants are usually tolerant of other animals, including other elephants. Here, antelope and elephants peacefully share a water hole.

Competing with Other Elephants

When competition between elephants occurs, it usually involves bull elephants competing for a mate. Bulls test their strength by sparring. They lock their tusks together and push at each other while they wrestle with their trunks. These mock fights are a way for male elephants to establish their rank among other bulls without risking serious injury.

When a bull is in musth, these fights can be serious. Musth makes bulls very aggressive, and they start to challenge other bulls for the chance to mate with females. They even challenge bulls that are much older and larger than they are. Sometimes the fights between bulls in musth can result in serious injury. Very rarely do these fights end in death.

When bulls spar, each elephant tries to push its rival back. If neither elephant moves, they stop, retreat a little, and come forward to push at each other again.

Relationships with Other Animals

Elephants are so large that most other animals try to avoid them. During a drought, all grazing animals find it difficult to find food. At these times, elephant activities may help other animals. By pulling down trees, they provide food for other herbivores who are not able to reach leaves and branches.

Sometimes a calf may fall prey to a large crocodile or a pride of lions. Usually, however, mother elephants are so watchful and protective of their young that such an event is rare. When a predator is close, an elephant family unit forms a loose circle, facing outward. The calves and youngsters are safe inside the circle. If a calf is taken by a predator, the adult elephants extend their ears and charge. This angry display usually succeeds in driving the predator away.

Predators rarely attack an adult elephant unless the elephant is injured or sick. However, elephant calves are more vulnerable. Nile crocodiles and lions are among the few predators that will prey on young elephants.

Competing with Humans

As human populations in Africa have grown, areas where elephants can live undisturbed have almost disappeared. Roads, villages, and farmland have steadily reduced elephant habitat.

As elephants travel in search of food and water, they use many traditional pathways that their families may have used for generations. In the last few decades, human populations have grown very quickly. Farms and villages have expanded into traditional elephant ranges. Sometimes these developments are built on or near an elephant pathway.

This means that elephants encounter many more villages and farms. As a result, many elephants have developed a taste for the crops that people have planted. When this happens, the elephants may raid fields and eat the crops. In many countries, crop-raiding elephants are shot. Elephants may succeed in driving off a pride of lions, but they are no match for a human with a gun.

Decline in Population

Many elephant populations in Africa and Asia are in decline for two reasons—habitat loss and hunting. Humans are responsible for both.

Human populations within elephant ranges are growing quickly. African and Asian elephants have lost much of their habitat to logging, cities, farms, and ranches. Some habitat loss is also caused by nature. In North Africa, elephants disappeared centuries ago from most of their historical territories because much of northern Africa became a desert. Only small populations of elephants in Namibia have managed to adapt to the hot, dry, desert climate.

The worst threat faced by African elephants once came from poaching. Elephants have been killed for their ivory since ancient times. The ivory trade was the greatest cause of elephant deaths in Africa in the 1970s and 1980s. Even elephants that lived in national parks were at risk. Most of the poaching ended with a 1989 international ban on the trade of ivory. Despite the ban, African elephant populations have been slow to recover. Elephant populations grow slowly because each elephant takes many years to reach maturity and breed.

At one time, buttons, piano keys, and billiard balls were made from ivory. Now there are many other materials that can be used to make these products. Roadside stands like this one in Tanzania are now illegal.

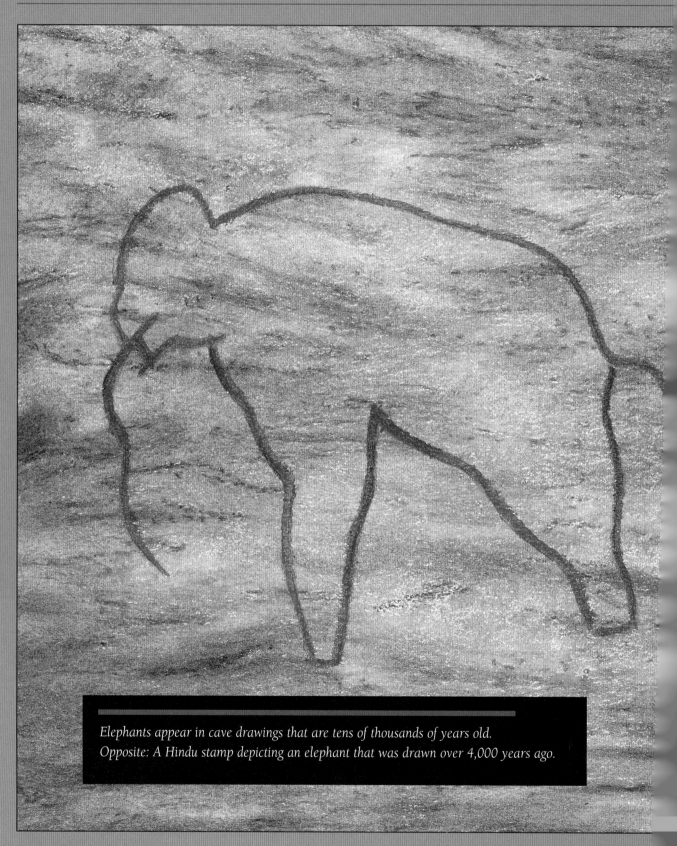

Elephants appear in cave drawings that are tens of thousands of years old.
Opposite: A Hindu stamp depicting an elephant that was drawn over 4,000 years ago.

Folklore

Folklore and myths are more than just stories. They reflect the way we feel about ourselves, the world, and the other creatures that live in the world with us. Elephants are worshipped in many Asian and African cultures. They symbolise intelligence, good luck, strength, happiness, and long life. In some cultures, small statues of elephants are placed in doorways. Some people believe that these elephant statues keep the household safe and free from evil. If the elephant's trunk is raised up, it is said that it will hold in good luck. An elephant statue with the trunk pointing down will let good luck escape.

Many ancient Asian cultures regarded the elephant as a divine animal. Today Asian elephants still play an important role in religious parades and festivals.

Folklore History

Gods with elephant heads are worshipped in India, Sri Lanka, South China, and Java. In Hindu mythology, the god of wisdom and good fortune is named Ganesha. Ganesha is portrayed as an elephant with a single tusk. According to legend, he used his other tusk to write the *Mahabharata*, an ancient epic that describes the conflict between two of India's great ruling families. Buddhists honoured white elephants because they believed that the animals had divine powers. The people of Siam also worshipped white elephants. Now called Thailand, their country's name once meant "Land of the Sacred White Elephant".

In Africa, elephants are symbols of good fortune and happiness. In some areas, cults were formed to honour the elephants that were killed by hunters. Some tribes believed that an elephant could be possessed by the spirit of an evil sorcerer. The sorcerer would then make the elephant trample crops and villages. In such cases, the evil sorcerer was blamed for the destruction rather than the elephant.

Ganesha is known as both the God of Wisdom and the Remover of Obstacles. Before starting any important task, Hindus call on Ganesha to make sure the job will go smoothly.

Myths vs. Facts

Elephants sleep standing up.

Elephants only sleep for 2 to 3 hours a day. Although an elephant may relax while standing up, most will lie down to sleep.

Pygmy elephants are miniature elephants that live deep in the forests of Africa.

The pygmy elephant, first described by a zoologist in 1906, was most likely a case of mistaken identity. Scientists now believe the pygmy was probably just a young forest elephant. At four years old, a forest elephant may show the same tusk development as a 10–15 year old bush elephant. People reporting pygmy elephants were probably just seeing young forest elephants, which are smaller, but more mature-looking than their bush elephant cousins.

When elephants are injured or sick, they go to a certain place to die. These "elephant graveyards" are filled with generations of elephant bones and tusks.

Elephant graveyards do not exist, except perhaps in places where hunters or poachers have killed whole families of elephants. Wounded or sick elephants die wherever their family unit happens to be at the time. The myth of graveyards may have begun because many elephant bones have been found near swamps. This has little to do with an elephant graveyard. Old elephants often die near swampy areas because they spend their final days eating the soft vegetation after their teeth have worn down.

Folktales

In folktales, the elephant is sometimes helpful, foolish, tricky, or even evil. Some stories try to explain things about the elephant, such as how it came to look the way it does, or why it lives in the hot grasslands. Here are a few tales you might enjoy:

Helpful Elephants

A king removes a thorn from an elephant's foot. Later the grateful elephant saves the king's son and the city from danger.

Wyatt, Isabel. *The Golden Stag and Other Folk Tales from India*. New York: McKay, 1962.

In "The Elephant's Lip" an elephant rescues girls from an evil witch.

Carpenter, Frances. *The Elephant's Bathtub: Wonder Tales from the Far East*. New York: Doubleday, 1962.

Elephant Adventure

Two children and an Indian elephant are pursued across America.

Cross, Gillian. *The Great Elephant Chase*. Oxford University Press, 1992.

Silly Stories

In "The Blind Men and the Elephant", four blind men feel an elephant to try to figure out what kind of creature it is.

Leach, Maria. *Noodles, Nitwits, and Numskulls*. Cleveland: World, 1961.

Evil Elephants

In the story, "Unanana and the Elephant", Unanana must rescue her family who has been eaten by an elephant.

Arnott, Kathleen. *African Myths and Legends*. Oxford University Press, 1989.